SOLO SPEECHES FOR

SOLO SPEECHES FOR UNDER-12s

Edited by Shaun McKenna

OBERON BOOKS
LONDON

First published in 1997 in association with the London Academy of
Music and Dramatic Art, by Oberon Books Ltd.
(incorporating Absolute Classics),
521 Caledonian Road, London N7 9RH
Tel: 020 7607 3637/Fax: 020 7607 3629
e-mail: oberon.books@btinternet.com

Reprinted 2000

Anthology copyright © The London Academy of Music and
Dramatic Art 1997

Copyright © contributions the contributors

All rights reserved. No reproduction, copy or transmission of this
publication may be made without written permission.

No paragraph of this publication may be reproduced, copied or
transmitted save with written permission or in accordance with the
provisions of the Copyright, Designs and Patents Act 1988, or under
the terms of any license permitting limited copying issued by the
Copyright Licensing Agency, Concept House, Cardiff Road, Newport,
South Wales, NP9 1RH.

Any person who does any unauthorised act in relation to this publication
may be liable to criminal prosecution and civil claims for damages.

This book is sold subject to condition that it shall not by way of trade or
otherwise be circulated without the publisher's consent in any form of
binding or cover other than that in which it is published and without a
similar conditon including that condition being imposed on any
subsequent purchaser.

A catalogue record of this book is available from the British Library.

ISBN: 1 84002 013 X

Cover design: Andrzej Klimowski

Cover typography: Richard Doust

Printed in Great Britain by Antony Rowe Ltd, Reading.

INTRODUCTION

This collection of pieces suitable for the under-12s will be found invaluable by Speech and Drama teachers looking for new material for examinations and festivals. All the pieces have been found effective in performance, and they come from a number of sources – full-length plays for children, theatre in education programmes, adaptations from classic books and folk tales from around the world.

They have been contributed by teachers, examiners and a number of professional writers, experienced in writing for this age group.

There is something for all age-groups and all tastes, and all selections are acceptable up to Junior Medallion in the LAMDA Examinations Acting syllabus.

So often, teachers complain that they are stuck using 'the same old pieces.' Many of the popular 'old faithfuls' will, of course, continue to be performed – and it is our earnest hope that some of the selections in this anthology will join them in the repertoire. Many of them are suitable for young actors of either sex.

Any of these pieces may be performed at festivals without permission being sought.

I wish you hours of pleasure and creative exploration with the material.

Shaun McKenna

CONTENTS

THE YELLOW ONE, *The Day The Colours Vanished*	Page 9
MARY, *Granny's Present*	Page 11
IZZY WIZZY, *Izzy Wizzy Gets Busy*	Page 13
IZZY WIZZY, *Izzy Wizzy Gets Busy*	Page 15
STATUE, *The Happy Prince*	Page 17
STAR, *Rairu and The Little Star*	Page 18
SISTER, *The Kacuy*	Page 20
SERVANT, *The Kitchen God*	Page 22
SAM, *Trouble At Home*	Page 24
SPIRIT OF THE LAKE, *The Seven Headed Serpent*	Page 26
THE WISE-WOMAN, *The Seven Headed Serpent*	Page 27
SARAH, *Catching Flies*	Page 29
THE WITCH-MAIDEN, *The Dragon of the North*	Page 31
PAT, *Food*	Page 33
BOLIVER, *The Enchanted Forest*	Page 35
JACK, *Detention*	Page 37
NIMMO, *The Dark Castle*	Page 38
ORGANIZITWELL, *King Panto's Violin*	Page 39
PILGRIM, *The Pilgrim*	Page 41
MAGGIE, *The Mill On The Floss*	Page 43
HANSA, *The Woodcutter's Daughter*	Page 45
JANE, *Jane Eyre*	Page 46
JANIE, *Eli's Scarf*	Page 47
POLLY, *Villette*	Page 49
MICHAEL, *Saturday*	Page 51
ROCKET, *The Remarkable Rocket*	Page 53
ROCKET, *The Remarkable Rocket*	Page 55
COMPA, *Playing With Fire*	Page 57
SAM, *All I Want Is Scruffy Back*	Page 59
DAVID, *The Bedroom*	Page 61
PRINCESS, *The Princess And The Swineherd*	Page 63
EMMA, *The Broken Ankle*	Page 65
MILLER, *The Devoted Friend*	Page 67
MILLER, *The Devoted Friend*	Page 69
LOU, *The Tooth Fairy*	Page 71
ANNIE, *Witches Incorporated*	Page 73

NELL, *The Old Curiosity Shop*	Page 75
DAVIE, *Making Friends*	Page 76
LAURIE, *Making Friends*	Page 77
BOY, *The Chimney Sweep's Boy*	Page 79
ALEXANDRA, *The Examination*	Page 81
TROUBLE, *Trouble*	Page 83
MARCELLUS, *At The Circus*	Page 85
EMMA, *Emma in 1848*	Page 87
JASON, *The Collector*	Page 89
PEARL, *The Scarlet Letter*	Page 91
JO, *I'm Cheesed Off*	Page 93
MARY, *The Secret Garden*	Page 94
BOY, *Tadpoles*	Page 96
HARRIET, *Ballet Exam*	Page 98
BOY, *The Cub's Trip*	Page 100

THE DAY THE COLOURS VANISHED

by Simon Patrick

It is Princess Crystal of Rainbowland's ninth birthday. She is given a coat made of all the colours of the rainbow but it is stolen from her by the wicked Grey Man. She sets off on a journey through Rainbowland, to get her colours back. The first person she meets is the bright, bouncing Yellow One. This scene can be played equally well by a boy or girl.

THE YELLOW ONE: Hello! What's the matter with you? You do look sad. Cheer up! (*Going closer.*) Please cheer up. There's nothing to cry about. Why, it's a lovely yellow day.

> I'm the jolly yellow one
> As cheerful as can be.
> If anybody's miserable
> They always come to me.
> I sing of sand and sunshine
> And haystacks piled up high.
> My song will make you smile again.
> It's easy if you try.

Come on, now. (*Has an idea.*) I know! Let me tell you a joke. Er.... What's yellow with black bits? (*Enthusiastic.*) Shark-infested custard, silly! (*Seeing her face.*) Oh, don't cry! I'll think of another one. Ummmm... What's long and bendy and yellow and yummy and has a feather on top? Don't you know? It's a banana with a hat on. (*Laughing wildly, then stopping as he sees her face.*) You don't like jokes very much do you? What if I make some funny faces? That'll cheer you up.

THE YELLOW FELLOW makes a series of funny faces, with appropriate noises to go with them – but the PRINCESS doesn't respond.

Oh dear, you are in a state, aren't you! (*Another idea.*) I know what we'll do. Why don't I give you some yellow. It's hard to be sad when you've got some yellow, because yellow's so.... (*A great whoop and a bounce.*) yellowish. Here, have my yellow hat. And have my yellow gloves. And my yellow belt.

The PRINCESS takes the clothes.

Put them on. How do you feel? Do you feel (*Bouncing a little.*) bouncy? I do. I'm always bouncing. Bounce, bounce, bounce – that's me! Come on, try doing a lovely yellow bounce with me. (*He starts bouncing, each bounce higher than the one before.*) Bounce... Bounce... BOUNCE!!!

Whee! I *knew* I could cheer you up.

GRANNY'S PRESENT

by Jeffrey du Cann Grenfell-Hill

The scene is set in Mary's bedroom. She is talking to a friend.

MARY: Have you seen Granny's latest present to me? We went down to see her at Easter. What a crush, sleeping-bags everywhere ... and in the middle of the night her cat came and jumped on top of me. What a fright I had! A purring black monster with yellow eyes. I gave the most terrible shriek, and everyone woke up. Well... I couldn't help it.

Granny likes to give me something special when I go down to visit. Last time it was a bonnet, one she had when she went gleaning ... you know like Biblical women, out in the fields picking up the ears of corn after the farmer had cut it. The women and girls still did that at harvest time when Gran was a girl. Her mother, that's my Great-Granny, used the gleanings for flour. It was back-breaking work, and they had large calico bonnets to shade their heads from the sun.

You'll be ever so jealous when you see my latest gift.

She holds out an old-fashioned doll.

Isn't she beautiful? A doll, Granny's favourite doll. She's still got all her original clothes. Look, a lace-trimmed petticoat and knickers ... don't laugh ... and I must be very careful with her china head. She's a museum piece, a real treasure. Gran said she had a wax-headed doll before this, but held it too near the fire, and it melted into a horrible mess. She cried and cried, until her sister Sarah promised to buy her a better one when she got her wages. And this is the doll! Bought in London... the best doll in the village. It's a family heirloom and now she's *mine!*

IZZY WIZZY GETS BUSY

by Simon Parker

Izzy Wizzy, a magician's apprentice, has been left behind by his master. The only person he has to talk to is his fellow-apprentice, Toad.

This scene could be played by a boy or a girl.

IZZY WIZZY: (*Whispering.*) Toad? Toad? Has he gone?

(*Breathing a sigh of relief.*) Oh, I am glad. Thank you for covering for me. If our master had found out it was me who put the treacle in the pig potion, he'd have turned me into a frog. Or a toad, like you. (*Laughing.*) It was funny though, wasn't it? How was I to know what would happen? I had just the tiniest taste of the pig potion and it was yuk. Absolutely Eeeergh. Completely blurrrh. I thought, 'This won't do. Nobody's going to drink this.' So I poured in half a tin of treacle. Who'd have thought it would make the pigs blow up like balloons, turn blue with yellow spots and float away out of the pig pen?

Toad, if only our master would let me learn proper magic out of his big black book, that sort of thing wouldn't happen, would it? I'd know what to expect. I mean, how hard can doing magic be? You've only got to pick the right sized wand, read the right words out of the book and wave your hands about a bit. Anybody could do it. *You* could do it.

What?

(*Giggling.*) No, we mustn't. We'll get into terrible trouble if he finds out. Do you really think we could? Oooh, how exciting. How thrilling. How jambamfantabulosible! Let's do it. Let's do a spell, our very own spell. Where's the big black book? Where's he hidden it? Hop over there and find it, Toad, while I get the wand.

What do you mean, get a small wand? Not me, not Izzy Wizzy. I'm going to get the biggest magic wand I can find!

IZZY WIZZY GETS BUSY

by Simon Parker

Izzy Wizzy, a scatterbrained magician's apprentice, hasn't learned much magic yet. But this does not stop him (or her) attempting a spell which is way beyond his capabilities.

Suitable for either a boy or a girl.

IZZY WIZZY: Pass me the book, Toad.

(*Awestruck.*) Look at this! The Grand High Wizard's very own spell book. And I'm going to do a spell from it. Me! Izzy Wizzy. I'm not stupid like everyone says. I'm a proper magician.

(*Flicking through pages.*) Now, Toad, what spell shall we do? There's one here to make someone's face turn into a custard tart. No. Oh, look! A growing spell. You can make whatever you want grow twelve feet tall. Would you like to be twelve feet tall, Toad? No? Alright.

(*Turns another page.*) The Grand High Wizard's Grand High Disappearing Spell. This sounds good. What shall we make disappear? What do we really hate? Shall we make the washing up disappear? Shall we make the Grand High Wizard disappear? That would be funny. No, I...

I know! What I hate most of all in the whole world is sums. I hate numbers. They never do what I tell them. I'm going to make all the numbers in the world disappear!

He strikes a pose with the wand, and reads from the book.

Allakazam, allakazoo,
This is the spell I'm going to do.

Allakazin, allakazon
All the numbers in the world be gone!
Now I make three passes with the wand.

He does so, with appropriate sounds.

(*With a flourish.*) Ka-bang!

Pause. He looks around.

Has anything happened?

THE HAPPY PRINCE

adapted by Jean Howell

Adapted from Oscar Wilde's children's story, the statue of the Happy Prince, set high in the town square, is talking to his new and only friend, the Swallow.

STATUE: I am the Happy Prince. When I was alive and had a human heart, I did not know what tears were, for I lived in the Palace of Sans-Souci, where sorrow is not allowed to enter. In the daytime I played with my companions in the garden, and in the evening I led the dance in the Great Hall. Round the garden ran a very lofty wall, but I never cared to ask what lay beyond it, everything about me was so beautiful. My courtiers called me the Happy Prince, and happy indeed I was, if pleasure be happiness. So I lived, and so I died. And now that I am dead they have set me up here so high that I can see all the ugliness and all the misery of my city, and though my heart is made of lead yet I cannot choose but weep. Far away, in a little street there is a poor house. One of the windows is open, and through it I can see a woman seated at a table. Her face is thin and worn, and she has coarse, red hands, all pricked by the needle, for she is a seamstress. She is embroidering passion-flowers on a satin gown for the loveliest of the Queen's maids-of-honour to wear at the next Court ball. In a bed in the corner of the room her little boy is lying ill. He has a fever, and is asking for oranges. His mother has nothing to give him but river water, so he is crying. Swallow, Swallow, little Swallow, will you not bring her the ruby out of my sword-hilt? My feet are fastened to this pedestal and I cannot move. You will stay with me for one night and be my messenger? Thank you, little Swallow.

RAIRU AND THE LITTLE STAR

by Simon Parker

Based on a South American folk tale, this tells of Rairu who lives in the middle of the rainforest. His mother and father have died and the only things he has to talk to are the flowers and the birds. One night, he lies out all night looking at the stars and decides he wants to talk to them, too. To his great surprise, a tiny young woman appears beside him.

STAR: Hello, Rairu. No, don't be afraid. I am your star, the star that you have been looking for. I am your own, very own, special star, Rairu. You must look after me.

Make me a bed, Rairu. Pluck down a calabash from that tree and scoop out the insides. Line it with soft, lovely moss. Then lay me down inside it, and cover me with soft turf so that no insects can bite me. Will you do that for me?

Oh yes, I knew you would. You will do anything to make me happy, won't you?

You say 'Yes' now and I can see that you mean it, and that you are happy. At this moment you love me, Rairu, I know that. But in time, you will forget me. I know you will. You will forget me, Rairu, and I shall have to return to my sisters in the sky.

Don't say too much, Rairu. I know you love me now. I love you, too. But you cannot promise that you will never forget me because you are human, and humans forget their promises more often than they keep them. But until you do forget me, I will live in this calabash and keep you company. I will tell you tales from the dark night sky. I will tell you of my sisters, the stars, and my aunts and uncles the planets and my mother the sun. I will tell you what it is like on the other side of the universe, further away than any human can even imagine. I will sing you songs, too, songs of such beauty that they make ordinary music sound like the wailing of a sick pig. And I will love you, Rairu. I will love you until you forget me.

THE KACUY

by Simon Parker

The kacuy is a South American bird, which gets its name from this legend. A boy, Kacuy, and his sister live together in a small village and she is so horrible to him that one day he tricks her into the high branches of a tall tree, where she is trapped. She calls his name but he will not go and fetch her, and eventually she turns into a bird. But she still calls his name from the high branches.

Here the sister is being horrible to Kacuy.

SISTER: It's alright for you, going out all day. I have to stay and look after the house. I should have a servant to do this. I shouldn't have to cook and clean and wash your clothes and do all the other things I have to do. Get me a servant!

What do you mean, you've brought me a present? What present? Flowers? Is that all? I don't want flowers, I want a proper present. Or a servant. Or a big bag of money. That would be more use than flowers.

I suppose you're starving, as usual. Because of you, I spend the whole day wearing my fingers to the bone. I cook you huge meals and you're still hungry. That big stomach never seems to get filled. Look at your stomach. You'll be fat soon, all the food you pile into it. And what thanks do I get? What thanks do I get?

Stop dreaming! Stop dreaming and listen to me! What thanks do I get, I asked you! I'll tell you. All the thanks I get is that miserable bunch of rotten little flowers. That's the way you thank me. I'm sick of you and I'm sick of this hut. I can't stand it any longer. You miserable, good-for-nothing creature, why can't you get me a better home? A girl like me should live in a palace and have servants of her own instead of being your slave.

(*Bursting into tears.*) I'm so unhappy. *I'm so unhappy!*

THE KITCHEN GOD

by Simon Parker

Based on a Chinese folk tale, this tells the story of poor stonemason who was once so short of money that he had to sell his wife to a rich merchant. Years later, the mason is called to the merchant's house to do some work. He does not recognise his former wife, but she takes pity on him. She bakes a basket of cakes and puts a gold coin in the middle of each one. But the mason, needing to pay his rent, sells the cakes for a single copper piece. He comes back to the merchant's house to return the empty basket.

This scene can be played by a young actor of either sex.

SERVANT: Hello, there. I didn't expect to see you again.

You're returning the basket? Thank you. (*She is about to go inside when she stops.*) Just a moment. Could I ask you something? Did you enjoy the cakes? My mistress made them specially.

You did eat them, didn't you? Alright, if you really did eat them, what was in them? Butter, flour, sugar, yes. What else? No, not currants, you silly man. What was in the middle of each cake?

No, not a plum. You didn't eat them, did you? Oh, my mistress will be so upset. She was trying to help you. Didn't you recognise her? She was your wife, the wife you sold to the merchant years and years ago. She recognised you at once, even though your hair has turned grey. And she felt so sorry for you, standing there in rags, all thin and sad-looking, that she baked those cakes with a gold coin in the middle of each one. There was a fortune in that basket of cakes. What did you do with it?

Whoever you sold it to got a pretty good bargain, I'd say. Why, he's probably built himself a fine big house in the centre of town with all that money.

Don't cry, you silly man. It's your own fault. If only you'd eaten even one of the cakes, and found out, it would have meant a happy ending for you. But now...

Oh, isn't it awful when things go wrong!

TROUBLE AT HOME

by Penny Phillips

Offstage is heard a slap. A scream. Feet running upstairs. A boy enters the room, slams the door and leans on it, sobbing and out of breath.

SAM: I hate her. I really hate her. Why does she have to be so horrible? (*Shouting downstairs.*) I hate you. I'm never going to come out again ... *ever!*

He slams the door again and stomps across to the window on the edge of the stage.

I wonder if I could get out of here. Where's the catch? Got it!

He lifts the sash window and looks out over the audience.

It's getting dark. (*Looking down.*) Oh, it's not too high up. I could sit on the edge of the porch. That will teach her. She'll think I've run away. She'll think I've jumped. She'll think I'm splattered on the road and a large lorry has run over me. Well, flat on the path, anyway! Hmm. I'll need to be comfy, and something to eat ... a pillow and ... where did I put those little Easter eggs.

Right, here goes.

He climbs out of the window onto the edge of the stage and the side-steps along with the pillow, bag of sweets and caterpault, improvising the problems and the noises.

Phew! Made it! Right ... Right, I'm here. This will teach her... I'm cold ... NO ... No, I'm not cold ... I'm not... She made me miss my tea. And my television! ... I can hear it. I hate her. When she comes looking for me, I'll shoot her with my caterpult. (*Looking around for a missile.*) What can I shoot at her? (*Fumbling in his pocket.*) I know, I'll use these tiny eggs: she gave them to me, she can have 'em back again! I bet they'll hurt.

He unwraps an egg and eats it.

It tastes funny. I wonder if she poisoned them ... Yuk!

He spits the egg out over the edge.

I feel sick. I bet she's polluted them. Oh no, I really do feel ill, my head's all swimmy. It's getting really dark. Maybe I'm going blind!

He sees someone coming up the garden path.

Mum! Mum! ... I'm up here, above the front door. Oh, Mum, Katy's been horrid to me again. She slapped me and I hate her! She poisoned my Easter eggs.

He listens for a moment.

It was because I put super glue on the dog. The vet's in the kitchen now. Mum, I'm sorry.

THE SEVEN HEADED SERPENT

by Simon Parker

This story is said to originate in the Greek island of Zakynthos. A king has decided to take a long voyage. He and his men land on an island where lions kill many of them. The survivors, running away, find a beautiful garden with a large lake. As soon as they reach the edge of it, the Spirit of the Lake rises up and speaks to them.

This spirit can be played by a boy or a girl.

SPIRIT OF THE LAKE: What are you doing here, my children, and whom do you seek? Are you come to visit our King?

You do well to be afraid, for you have put yourselves in danger by coming here. Our king, who has seven heads, is now asleep, but in a few minutes he will rise up and come to this lake to take his bath. It will be a grave mistake if you are still here, for if he meets anyone in his garden, he will kill them and eat them. Listen! I think I hear him yawning. He must be awake.

This is what you must do if you want to survive. Take off your cloaks and spread them on the path which leads from here to the palace. The King will then have something soft to glide on, which is something he very much likes. If you do what I say, he will be so pleased that he will not devour you. He will punish you, certainly, but he will let you go.

Listen! Can you hear that hissing? He is coming. Our King is not a man, as you are, he is a serpent, a great seven headed serpent. Off with your cloaks now! Hurry! Hurry! There is not a moment to lose.

THE SEVEN HEADED SERPENT

by Simon Parker

This Greek folk tale is similar to the famous tale of Theseus and the Minotaur. Because of an arrangement made by the King to save his life, every year twelve youths and twelve maidens must sail to a distant island to be devoured by the fearsome Seven-headed Serpent. When the King dies, his son visits an old wise-woman who may be able to help him defeat the evil serpent.

THE WISE-WOMAN: What is it you want with me? Leave me to my spinning. I have been sitting here for years and years, spinning my thread, seeing no by visitors. I want no visitors now. Be off with you!

What's that? You are the Prince? Well, why didn't you say so? I told your mother before you were born that you were the only hope for lifting the curse. And now you are come to find out how. How old are you? Hmmm. You look rather puny and pathetic for your age.

It's a good job I have something special up my sleeve, isn't it? A good job I have a little magic. Yes, magic. How else do you expect to defeat a Seven-headed Serpent?

Take this ointment, this little jar. Load your horse with cotton wool, and rub this ointment on your horse's muzzle. It will take him by a secret path, a path only I know about, that leads straight to the Serpent's palace. You will find the Serpent asleep on his bed, which is hung all round with bells. Over the bed you will see a sword hanging. Only with this sword is it possible to kill the Serpent, because even if it breaks, a new blade will grow again for every head the monster has. Thus you will be able to cut off all seven heads.

What do you mean, what is the cotton wool for? I've told you. Haven't I told you? Well, you don't want the bells to ring and wake up the monster, do you? Take the cotton wool into the bedchamber and wrap every bell in it. That way you can give the monster the surprise of his life.

That's all. Go now. I have spinning to do.

CATCHING FLIES

by Penny Phillips

Sarah is very small and serious and very nice – most of the time. She is staring intently at a fly that is flying in front of her and settles on the window pane – the audience are the window. Sarah speaks with a bunged-up nose as if she has a cold. She creeps up to the fly. Just as she is about to grab it she gives an enormous sniff.

SARAH: Missed it!

Katie Saunders can catch flies as easy as anything.

She watches carefully, slowly creeps closer – then sniffs and grabs.

Darn it! I need a really slow one. (*Sniff.*) Oh, I'm fed up. (*Sniff.*) I'm fed up with everyone copying me... (*Sniff.*) I can't help sounding bunged up, it's my adenoids.

She freezes as she sees a fly, watches, sniffs, grabs.

And I'm fed up with Miss Roberts saying (*Imitating her.*) 'Do shut your mouth, Sarah. Are you catching flies? Ha ha ha.' She says it every day and laughs that funny horsey laugh. I don't say to her, 'What a funny laugh, Miss Roberts. Have you swallowed a horse?'

(*Seeing a fly.*) There's a big fat slow one. I'll hold my breath...

She takes a deep breath, creeps, concentrates and catches it.

Got it! I've caught one! I've really caught one! Just wait till tomorrow! When she says, 'Sarah, are you catching flies?' I'll open my hand right under her nose and let this out and say, 'Yes, Miss Roberts. *Look!*'

She opens her hand wide, to demonstrate. The fly flies away.

Oh, I give up!

Sniff.

THE DRAGON OF THE NORTH

by Simon Parker

This story comes from Estonia in Eastern Europe. A youth, searching for the magic ring which will defeat a terrible dragon, has spent the night by a lake. A beautiful maiden has come out of the depths of the forest and taken him back to her home. She takes him to a secret chamber.

THE WITCH-MAIDEN: I am young and beautiful and I am no man's slave. Until now, I have never thought of marrying, but the moment I saw you, I began to change my mind. So, if you feel the same, we could be man and wife. I am very rich indeed. We could live like kings. Whatever you want, I can get for you.

I see you need time to think. Let me show you something which might help you make up your mind. See, this silver box. Inside it is a precious gold ring. When you marry me, I will give you this ring as a marriage gift. It will make you the happiest of human men. But in order that our love may last forever, before I give you the ring you must give me three drops of blood from the little finger of your left hand.

What is special about the ring? No human can fully understand its power because no human can read the secret signs engraved on it. Even with my half-knowledge, I can work wonders. If I put the ring on the little finger of my left hand, I can fly through the air like a bird. On the middle finger, it makes me invisible – imagine how useful that can be! If I wear it on the third finger, neither fire nor water nor any sharp weapon can hurt me. On the first finger, it enables me to conjure up whatever I want – from a palace to a fine meal. On my left thumb, it makes my hand so strong that it can break through rocks and smash through walls.

I see you are interested. Who knows what powers *you* will discover, once you possess the ring.

FOOD

by Jeffrey du Cann Grenfell-Hill

This original speech is suitable for either sex.

Pat is talking to a schoolfriend, while doing some homework. The performer could also mime eating or watching TV.

PAT: All this talk about junk food... well, let's get one thing straight, I like junk food, crisps, chips, beef-burgers, what's wrong with 'em. And white bread, why can't I have sliced white bread from the supermarket? It's all food isn't it? But no... Mum's into high fibre diets, it's enough to kill you... wholemeal bread, great big chunks of it... yuck! And no-one's allowed butter any more... that's supposed to be a real killer.

Well... my Mum made Dad give up smoking 'cos it's a killer an' he did it, just to please 'er... now he's got to give up butter, cheese, streaky bacon and cream puddings... they're all killers... How the human race has survived so far I'll never know... My gran says she's not giving up butter even if it is going to kill 'er... but I reckon at seventy-eight she's got to be immune to whatever it is what kills you in butter.

We get all these colour magazines about health foods. If I see another bean salad I'm going to be sick all over the place... yuck... and jacket potatoes covered in yoghurt... yuck... Gran an' me we sneak down to the chippy an' get a great big bag of chips... she meets me after Youth Club...

Mum's now counting cups of coffee... we're only allowed one cup after each meal 'cos more is supposed to be bad for you... Gran spends most of her time down the cafe drinking cups of coffee an' smoking herself silly between cream cakes... I bet she regrets coming to live with us... but then, that was before Mum got hooked on high fibre... I wonder how long before all these killers get to Gran?

THE ENCHANTED FOREST

by Simon Patrick

An old woman has followed her straying hens into the forest, where she has become lost. She sees a large bird with colourful feathers and is very surprised when it starts to speak with her.

Suitable for a young performer of either sex.

BOLIVER: Coo-coo, coo-coo. It's no good going that way, you know. There's nothing down there except... well, let's just say you don't want to go that way. Coo-coo.

Coo. My name is Boliver, coo-coo. And there's no need to look quite so surprised. This *is* The Enchanted Forest, you know.

What? You didn't know it was The Enchanted Forest? Are you new to the neighbourhood? Or are you just deaf, coo-coo-coo? Don't be offended. You're an old woman, you might very well be deaf. Coo-coo. All sorts of things happen to people in *here.* I was talking to the Water Buffalo the other day, coo-coo – he's very nice but he's a wee bit grumpy – and he told me that the Phoenix went for a walk the other day, and when it came back, all its feathers had turned completely white.

The Phoenix went *that* way, you see. The way you were going. I wouldn't try it, if I were you. Mind you, you wouldn't have to worry about your hair going white – it's white already – coo-coo, coo-coo, coo-coo.

What's actually *down* there? Nobody knows. Nobody who has been there can ever bring themselves to speak about it. All I can say is – down there is something that's *not very nice.* Something not natural. Something that belongs to... *her!*

(*In alarm.*) Coo-coo, coo-coo. Don't ask me to say *her* name! She'll hear if I say her name, wherever she is, and then she'll... Coo-coo, coo-coo... Please go away, old woman. I've said too much already.

DETENTION

by Felicity Blackstone

Jack, an easy-going lad on the whole, would probably prefer to be out on the football pitch than in class.

JACK: Guess where I am? In detention with Rajiv beside me. A two hundred word essay on why I must not eat in class. Two hundred words! I can't think of anything to write.

All right, so break is the time for scoffing chocolate bars according to Old-Crow-Face, Mr Crowley, our French teacher. But what would you do if your tummy was rumbling in the middle of conjugating the verb to eat? It was the mere mention of the word that set it off. The notes it was churning out were not dissimilar to the Marseillaise. Most appropriate, I thought. Anyway, Rajiv started to get the giggles. At this point Mr. Crowley Crow suddenly lost his temper and sent my poor friend out of the class and told him to make up the work in detention.

Well, to stop any more eruptions from either my stomach or Crow-Face I considered that the best approach was to secrete my chocolate mallow bar into my mouth in bite sized portions. I was just enjoying my third portion when he pounced on me to translate 'the boy eats the biscuit' into French. Unfortunately, at this point I choked on my chocolate bar... (*He sighs.*)

No lying in tomorrow I suppose .... I'll have to get up in time for some breakfast. (*Starting to write.*) I must not eat in class because ...

THE DARK CASTLE

by Simon Parker

Nimmo, a troll, has been imprisoned in a dark dungeon by the villainous Count Fosco. But now someone has opened the dungeon door...

This troll can be played by a boy or a girl.

NIMMO: Oh master! My grand, brave master. Is it suppertime? I *am* hungry, oh yes I am. So hungry... Please feed me, master.

What? Who's there? You're not my master. Who... who are you?

Get away from me! This is a trick, I know it is. My master has sent you to see if I'm loyal to him. I *am* loyal to the brave Count Fosco. The fearsome Fosco is the greatest, grandest, gorgeousest master in the whole world. You'll tell him I said that, won't you? You *will* tell him?

What? What are you saying? Don't say that, he'll hear you. He knows everything that goes on in his kingdom, every little thing. Why, if he heard you say that he'd...

Hang on a minute. He *didn't* send you, did he? He really didn't. Have you come to rescue me? Have you? Oh, I've waited months and months to be rescued from his horrible, hateful hole. Who are you? What's your name?

Princess Ira? Not *the* Princess Ira? Fosco told us all that you were dead. Dead! (*Panicking.*) You're a ghost, aren't you? You're a ghost and you've come to haunt me. (*Shrieking.*) Aaargh!

Oh, why does nothing good ever happen to *me*.

KING PANTO'S VIOLIN

by Jeffrey du Cann Grenfell-Hill

In this scene, set in a market square, the King's Secretary has an important announcement to make. Organizitwell could be played by either a boy or a girl. Organizitwell is rather pompous. A suggestion of costume might help.

ORGANIZITWELL: Line them up, guards, line them up. That's it, straight lines, hats off. Now the king has ordered that every male over the age of sixteen must be interrogated. Why? You mean you don't know? This morning, as King Panto was playing his violin, he put it down in the Royal Rose Garden, and lo and behold, after he'd finished blowing his nose (Very particular he is about his nose.), it had gone. *Gone!* His magic violin not his nose. It plays in tune however awful the royal fingers stumble, perfect tune. Mozart it plays, Beethoven, Schu...ah! Well your sort of person wouldn't know, would you? Keep in line, keep in line.

The king was so upset, he couldn't eat his usual breakfast of four bowls of chocolate chips with orange sauce, four pieces of Black Forest Gateau and two wedges of fruit cake. Instead, he only managed a box of Turkish Delight and a strawberry milkshake. Now, he has commissioned me to find the thieves who stole the Royal violin. Who am I? You mean, nincompoops, you don't know who I am? I am Organizitwell, the Royal Secretary. You will all address me as Your Secretaryship.

Now, who will be first with information? Come on, someone must know something. If you don't come forward the king will close all the discos... he will close all the chippies... he will... Come on, confess!

Oh, yes! I forgot to say, there's a £100 reward. Ah! Don't all stampede, stop shouting... one at a time, one at a time please.

Falls to the ground besieged by informants.

THE PILGRIM

by Simon Parker

This is based on The Voyage of Maelduin, *an ancient Irish legend. It tells of Maelduin, the son of a chieftain murdered by maruarding bandits. For safety's sake, Maelduin was brought up in the queen's household as one of the royal children. Discovering his true identity, he set off by sea to find the men who murdered his father. Maelduin visited many islands and had many adventures. On one isolated island, he comes upon an ancient Pilgrim whose hair has grown so long and thick that he made clothes from it.*

The scene can be played equally well by a boy or a girl.

PILGRIM: There's nothing funny about the way I look, young man. How rude!

You see, I'm so old and my hair has grown so long that it seems plain silly to wear clothes. What I do is this: every time my hair grows another few inches, I get two twigs and knit it into clothes. Look, I've got trousers and a nice shirt – all made out of my own hair, and all still connected to my head.

A long time ago, young Maelduin, I came from Ireland. When I was small, my dear mother took me to church every day and I became very religious. One day I took it into my head to go and visit one of the great holy shrines. I made a raft out of skins – made it with my own hands, I did. But I wasn't very good with my hands then, not like I am now, and it wasn't long before the raft started letting in water. I was really frightened. I thought it would overturn and I'd be drowned, so I paddled back to land. I cut some squares of turf from a field to mend the holes in my raft. I set out again – but the raft still wasn't very good. I was miles from anywhere and sinking fast. So I prayed. I prayed and prayed. God was listening that day, that's for sure. The turfs floated off my raft and turned into this island! It was a miracle. Every year, my island gets a foot bigger all round. I've got a fountain of beer just outside my hut and angel cakes grow from the trees.

Don't you believe me?

THE MILL ON THE FLOSS

adapted by Judith Wilson

Adapted from George Eliot's classic novel, which tells the story of the childhood and young adulthood of the Tulliver family. Here, Maggie Tulliver, aged about eight, is talking to her elder brother, Tom, whom she idolises. He has just returned from the academy boarding school and presents her with a new fishing-line. She has to confess some bad news about his rabbits which she has neglected during his absence. The setting is Lincolnshire in 1829.

MAGGIE: Oh, you're a good brother to me, Tom, to buy me a line all to myself. I do love you, Tom, and you're so brave. I think you're like Samson. If there came a lion roaring at me, I think you'd fight him, wouldn't you, Tom? I mean, if we were in the lion countries, I mean in Africa, where it's very hot – the lions eat people there. I can show it to you in the book where I read it. We might have gone out, you know, not thinking – just as we go fishing; and then a great lion might run towards us roaring, and we couldn't get away from him. What should you do, Tom? I like to fancy how it would be...

Tom? Where are you going?... To the rabbits?... Tom, how much money did you give for your rabbits?... Two half crowns and sixpence?... I think I've got a great deal more than that in my steel purse upstairs. I'll ask Mother to give it to you out of my purse to put into your pocket and spend. You could buy some more rabbits with it... Tom, they're all dead. Oh, Tom, I know you told me to be sure and remember the rabbits every day, but how could I when they did not come into my head?

Yes, I forgot, and I couldn't help it indeed, Tom. I'm so very sorry. Oh Tom, I'd forgive you if you forgot anything. I wouldn't mind what you did. I'd forgive you and love you. Oh please, forgive me Tom, my heart will break... (*TOM exits.*) Oh he is so cruel!

THE WOODCUTTER'S DAUGHTER

by Allan Wilkins

A dramatisation from a Norwegian folk tale, similar to the English story of Red Riding Hood.

Hansa has gone out into the forest to look for flowers. It is the first time she has wandered so far, and she is lost. Her mother has always warned about going too far away from home as there are strange stories of what goes on in the woods.

HANSA: Don't stay long in the wood, mother said. Now look what's happened? I'm lost! That kind old lady said take the third path on the left. I did that, but that seems to have led me nowhere. (*She sits.*) It's getting dark... I'm cold... and I'm hungry. (*A twig snaps.*) What's that? Who's there? It must have been an animal. I don't like this place. It's as though... something or someone was watching you. Is there anybody there? No-one.

At least that kind old lady gave me an apple. I shan't starve. (*Stopping herself from taking a bite.*) Mother said never take things from strangers ... but there can't be anything wrong with an apple, can there? No, of course not, that's silly! (*Takes a bite.*) Um, delicious! It's funny how that lady just disappeared. One minute she was there and when I turned round she'd gone. I was just about to ask if... (*She suddenly feels faint.*) ... that's funny... I feel dizzy... I... it must be the apple... the old lady... what has she done...?

She falls and stumbles along. Then she looks up and sees the old lady standing in front of her.

You!... What have you done?... You've poisoned me... help... someone help me... please don't hurt me... (*She faints.*)

JANE EYRE

adapted by Jacqueline Emery

Adapted from Charlotte Bronte's famous novel, this scene shows Jane – a young orphan living in a loveless home – punished by being locked in 'the red room' in which her uncle died.

JANE: Let me out! Let me out! I won't say my prayers. I won't! I won't! I don't care if Miss Abbott is right and something bad does come down the chimney to take me away. I really wish it would, then I wouldn't have to live in this horrible house again. But... I don't think it will and I'm scared. Scared of this lonely, cold bedroom; scared of those shadows and those flickering lights. Oh, my head is aching so much after that fall! It just isn't fair to lock me away in here. If Uncle Read had been alive he would never have allowed them to be so hard and cruel to me. Oh, why did they do it? Why?

Oh! There's a light on the wall and it's moving towards me. Oh look, the shadows and the lights... they seem to be moving across the room. They're coming closer. They're closing in on me. Help! Help! Bessie! Aunt! I can't bear it any longer! Let me out! Let me out! Please open the door. Please take me out. Let me go to the nursery. I'm afraid. Let me hold your hand, Bessie. Please don't turn away from me. Oh aunt, have pity. Forgive me! I can't endure it. Let me be punished some other way.

ELI'S SCARF

by Raechelle Reid

adapted by Priscilla Morris

American – Deep South. Janie is a shy girl with a naive faith in human nature. She is described as 'slow' mentally and is talking directly to the audience.

JANIE: This was my brother's scarf. He gave it to me. His name was Eli – Eli Johnson and I loved him so much...

My Momma died when I was born so I never knowed her. One time I heard my Poppa saying to Eli, "If Janie hadn't been born then Kitty would have been with us today. She ought never to have been born, not ever!" I don't think Poppa meant for me to hear how much he hated me, but I did, and it hurt me somewhere deep inside.

Anyway, I tried to be happy and Eli helped me. He took me hunting and taught me how to shoot. One day I was going to meet him at our special meeting place and I had on the scarf which was keeping me nice and snug. Suddenly I saw Eli lying on the ground and I called out, "Come on, you lazy varmint, we're goin' out huntin'." It wasn't 'till I got close that I saw the blood...

Now I may be a little bit slow sometimes but I know what a dead man looks like. His eyes looked up at me real funny.

Well, I cried out and I ran home as fast as I could to tell Poppa. I shouted, "Poppa, it's Eli, someone's shot him and he's dead, come quick!" Then it was real strange... Poppa didn't scream or shout, he just laughed... he laughed and said, "You don't know nothing girl... you didn't see nothin', do you understand?" Then he came towards me and I was real frightened so I ran... I ran away as fast as I could until I got here. Now I'm alone, there ain't no one to love me no more and I don't know what I'm gonna do but I still got Eli's scarf and I guess that will always keep me warm.

VILLETTE

adapted by Jean Howell

This passage is adapted from Chapter Three of Charlotte Bronte's classic novel. Polly, a young and sensitive child, her mother dead and her father recuperating abroad, is left in the care of kindly Mrs Bretton. Graham Bretton, her son, gives Polly a doll which she names Candace. In this speech, Polly confides in Mrs Bretton's goddaughter, Lucy Snowe.

POLLY: Miss Snowe, this is a wonderful book. Candace is asleep now, and I may tell you about it; only we must both speak low, lest she should waken. This book was given me by Graham; it tells about distant countries, a long, long way from England, which no traveller can reach without sailing thousands of miles over the sea. Wild men live in these countries, Miss Snowe, who wear clothes different from ours: indeed, some of them wear scarcely any clothes, for the sake of being cool, you know; for they have very hot weather. Here is a picture of thousands gathered in a desolate place – a plain, spread with sand – round a man in black – a good, good Englishman – a missionary, who is preaching to them under a palm-tree. And here are pictures more stranger then that. There is the wonderful Great Wall of China; here is a Chinese lady, with a foot littler than mine. There is a wild horse of Tartary; and here, most strange of all – is a land of ice and snow, without green fields, woods, or gardens. In this land, they found some mammoth bones: there are no mammoths now. You don't know what it was; but I can tell you, because Graham told me. A mighty, goblin creature, as high as this room, and as long as the hall; but not a fierce, flesh-eating thing, Graham thinks. He believes, if I met one in a forest, it would not kill me, unless I came quite in its way; when it would trample me down amongst the bushes, as I might tread on a grasshopper in a hayfield without knowing it.

SATURDAY

by Felicity Blackstone

Michael is normally perky, with a lively sense of humour. Now he is down in the dumps.

MICHAEL: I'm bored. Nothing's gone right today. If I had known what sort of day it was going to be I probably wouldn't even have bothered getting out of bed. The weather has changed. All week while we have been slaving away at school, the sun has shone brightly outside. Today is Saturday and it's raining. I was all ready to play football in the first elevens against our greatest rivals, the Wanderers. Yes, I had actually been picked at last for the first eleven. I was going out there to prove that they should have picked me instead of Jim right at the beginning of the season instead of waiting until now. But what happens? There's a 'phone call first thing this morning from Bob, our coach, to say he's very sorry but the pitch is waterlogged and so the game has been called off. Well you can imagine my feelings.

Right, I thought, this is not going to get me down, I'll call up my friend Jake and he can come over and we can play Lemmings on the computer. His mother tells me that Jake has to meet his aunt who is over from New Zealand.

Then I had the brilliant idea. I would complete my model kit of the harrier. It's been sitting in the box half-made for ages. Well, I cleared my desk of all the junk and laid out all the bits. The harrier was coming along fine. All it needed was the undercarriage wheels to be put in place. As I prised them off the plastic frame one of the wheels flew off across the room somewhere in the direction of my bed. I searched for it everywhere. It was not to be found. Just not my day.

I'm bored.

THE REMARKABLE ROCKET

adapted by Priscilla Morris

Oscar Wilde's enchanting short story about a very pompous firework is full of lively and amusing characters. Here, the boastful rocket is fixed to a board with other fireworks for a grand display at the Prince and Princess's wedding.

ROCKET: I am a remarkable rocket, and come from remarkable parents. My mother was the most celebrated Catherine wheel of her day, and was renowned for her graceful dancing. When she made her great public appearance she spun round nineteen times before she went out, and each time she threw into the air seven pink stars. My father was a rocket like myself. He flew so high that the people were afraid that he would never come down again. He did, though, and made a most brilliant descent in a shower of golden rain. The newspapers wrote about his performance in glowing terms.

The CRACKER begins giggling.

Pray, what are you laughing at? I am not laughing. What right have you to be happy? You should be thinking about others. In fact, you should be thinking about me. I am always thinking about myself, and I expect everybody else to do the same. None of you have any hearts. Here you are, laughing and making merry just as if the Prince and Princess had not been married.

Just think – perhaps they may go to live in a country where there is a deep river, and perhaps they may have only one son, a little fair-haired boy with violet eyes like the Prince himself; and perhaps someday he may go out to walk with his nurse; and perhaps the nurse may go to sleep under a great elder-tree; and perhaps the little boy may fall into the deep river and be drowned. What a terrible misfortune! Poor people, to lose their only son! It really is too dreadful! I shall never get over it!"

He starts to sob noisily.

THE REMARKABLE ROCKET

adapted by Jean Howell

This episode takes place at the end of Oscar Wilde's story about the bombastic Rocket when he has been lit but fizzled out and fallen into a midden.

ROCKET: I am merely a visitor, a distinguished visitor. The fact is that I find this place rather tedious. There is neither society here, nor solitude. In fact, it is essentially suburban. I shall probably go back to Court, for I know that I am destined to make a sensation in the world. I am made for public life and so are all my relations, even the humblest of them. Whenever we appear we excite great attention. I have not actually appeared myself, but when I do so it will be a magnificent sight. As for domesticity, it ages one rapidly, and distracts one's mind from higher things.

Oh, these two boys must be the deputation.

'*Old Stick!*' one called me. Impossible! *Gold Stick*, that is what he said. Gold Stick is very complimentary. In fact, he mistakes me for one of the court dignitaries! They are putting me on the fire to boil the kettle! This is magnificent, they are going to let me off in broad daylight, so that every one can see me. Now I am going off! I know I shall go much higher than the stars, much higher than the moon, much higher than the sun. In fact, I shall go so high that...

Fizz! Fizz! Fizz! Delightful! I shall go on like this for ever. What a success I am! Now I am going to explode, I shall set the whole world on fire, and make such a noise that nobody will talk about anything else for a whole year.

Bang! Bang! Bang!

I knew I should create a great sensation.

The ROCKET goes out.

PLAYING WITH FIRE

by Priscilla Morris

The setting is prehistoric. In a clearing in a wood, a Chief and his tribesmen sit in a circle ready to try a man and his son accused of a terrible crime! The medicine man, Compa, comes forward.

This piece is suitable for either sex.

COMPA: Oh great Chief! I have to tell you of a horrible and unnatural deed which has taken place this day. You know, great one, that I can see all things. I live alone in my cave but nothing is hidden from me. When the young men of the tribe go out to hunt the great wild beasts, I can see the chase and the kill although I am not with them. It is I who brings the glad tidings to the women of the tribe before the swiftest warrior returns. If the old men whisper together secretly in the darkness, I hear their plots – and many have lived to regret the words they spoke!

Why do the warriors stand back and the women stop their chatter when I, Compa, come near? They are afraid, for I can see the evil in their hearts!

He glances round and some of the tribesmen look uncomfortable.

I smell out the bad and now, oh great one, my nostrils have smelt a strange smell indeed! A burning smell – a foul smell – an unhealthy smell! And do you know where it came from? Why the house of Kumba and his son.

In the winter – when we sit around our caves and warm our feet in the embers – we are thankful for the great gift of fire, but this ungrateful Kumba and his thoughtless son have abused that gift by doing a truly dreadful thing. Tribesmen – I ask you to bear witness that they have been guilty of eating the flesh of pig – *burnt with fire!*

Cries of detestation and horror.

There is only one judgement you can bring and I ask you to do so. *Now!*

ALL I WANT IS SCRUFFY BACK

by Jeffrey du Cann Grenfell-Hill

The scene is set anywhere; it is a chat amongst friends about a missing dog. The speech will suit either a boy or a girl. This scene works well if mimed as taking place in a school canteen – queing for dinner, finding a place to sit and eating while talking to a friend.

SAM: He wouldn't just wander off, not Scruffy... Mum didn't like him the minute I brought him home. "Nasty, scruffy little mongrel," she said... "Dogs smell the place up," she said. I suppose from the very beginning I should have known she had it in for him. "Get that dog off your bed," she'd say, "he's got fleas." But he didn't really, except for one or two, and what's one or two on a dog that's part Labrador and part Irish Setter? Nothing. Then when he started stealing things... You see, he was so big, he could rest his head on the dinner table. One Sunday I saw him lick the entire joint of lamb, all over, while Mum was making the gravy, but I never said anything. We all ate it an' lived. But it was last Sunday that did it, when he munched up the entire chicken when Mum was mashing the potatoes... By the time she'd got through, all she found was a wing on the carpet behind the sofa. I didn't mind having just vegetables for dinner, but the others moaned a bit, and Mum was so hysterical she spent the rest of the day in bed. It must have been because while we were eating our mashed potatoes he went into the kitchen and ate the apple crumble.

I think Mum gave Dad an ultimatum... "It's either that dog or me!" You know, emotional blackmail – the sort of trick people use when moaning and groaning hasn't worked. Well, Dad took about three days to think about it... He's not the sort of man to act on impulse, or when he's being bossed... and Mum must have got a bit impatient. Yesterday she said he started having fits, frothing at the mouth he was (Scruffy I mean, not Dad). Mum said she got really frightened. "What if he bites somebody?" she said. "He'd kill somebody if he went into a mad fit." So now he's gone. When I came home from school, he wasn't there... Mum was, having a cup of tea, and smiling quietly to herself...

"Give us a kiss," she said. But I couldn't, I just couldn't.

All I want... is Scruffy back.

THE BEDROOM

by Felicity Blackstone

At the start of this scene, David is shouting down the stairs to his mother.

DAVID: What's wrong with my bedroom, Mum? I like it this way. I know where everything is. I've made a pathway to my bed so nothing will get trodden on and broken. Don't worry about getting the vacuum over the carpet – a little bit of dust doesn't do any harm.

Oh, all right then. All right, I'll tidy it. (*Mutters.*) Anything for a quiet life.

He opens a drawer, starts picking up bits.

In you go. I suppose that I'll have to put these soldiers away. I was in the middle of setting them up for a battle. It was going to be against the Warlords. I had planned a really good game there... In you all go.

He picks up a magazine and starts to read it.

What's this? A competition to win a trip on Concorde for the day – great! I've always wanted to fly in Concorde, I've seen it enough time flying over the house and I've always envied those lucky passengers inside. Imagine travelling faster than the speed of sound and being in New York in time for lunch.

What do I have to do? (*Reads.*) Make five words out of the word CONCORDE. That should be easy enough... First of all there's C-O-N "con" and C-O-R-D "cord"; they're easy. Now for three more words... Ah! D-O-O-R "door" good! and D-O-N "don". Just one more, let's see... um... yes! C-O-R-N "corn". What are the instructions? (*Reads.*) 'Write your answers clearly on a postcard with your name and address and send to the above address to arrive not later than October 1st.' October 1st! That was last month. Surely the magazine hasn't been lying on the floor that long!

Perhaps Mum is right about my room after all.

THE PRINCESS & THE SWINEHERD

by Priscilla Morris

This popular fairy-tale by Hans Christian Andersen tells the story of a proud princess who, refusing all her suitors, is married off to a swineherd and learns humility. As in all good fairy tales, the swineherd turns out to be a prince who truly loves her.

In this scene, the Princess is found playing ball with two attendants.

PRINCESS: Oh, you stupid, stupid thing! That is the third time you have missed your throw. What did you say? Of course it was straight; Princesses always throw straight, don't they? Now don't stand chattering; begin again, and remember, after this, the first who misses shan't play anymore.

The Princess misses.

(*Angrily.*) There! That was your fault; you can't throw straight, either of you. It's a silly game anyway so go away and leave me alone!

The Emperor enters.

Good day father. I suppose it's nearly time for me to meet another of your boring Princes. Why do you keep inviting them? They are none of them good enough. The last one had too big a nose and couldn't speak without gobbling like a turkey. His Kingdom was such a little one and his palace wasn't a palace at all, only a plain, ordinary castle with not more than a hundred servants in it. Besides I don't want to get married, so you can tell this new Prince to go away for I won't see him!

What did you say? Has he brought me a present?
Oh I do hope it's a little cat! I've always wanted
one. Open it! Open it quickly!

The EMPEROR opens the present.

Why, it's nothing but an ordinary flower – what a
common thing! You can take it away again. Tell the
Prince I won't marry him, so he needn't bother to
wait. Now go, father, and leave me alone – I am
tired of silly presents and Princes!

THE BROKEN ANKLE

by Felicity Blackstone

Emma is a bright girl, full of energy and determination. Her friends have run on ahead of her.

EMMA: (*Shouts.*) Hey, you two, wait for me!

They have not listened to her.

It's not fair! Just because I'm the youngest and smallest, they never want me in their games – well, I'm going to catch up with them. I know where they've gone. (*Starting to run.*) Wait for me!

She trips and falls.

Ow! Oh no! that's done it, my new jeans have got a rip in them. I only got them last weekend – how annoying, Mum will be furious. (*Trying to get up.*) Ouch, my ankle; it really hurts. What have I done to it? I can't walk on it. Oh bother, I'd better sit down again. Let's have a look at it. (*Pulling up her trouser leg.*) It's not bleeding or anything but it looks swollen. (*Prodding it.*) Ooh, that hurts! What shall I do? Perhaps I can try hopping along on the other leg.

She struggles to her feet and tries – but it is no good.

I'm never going to get back home like this. Maybe I can try crawling on my good leg and dragging my other leg. (*She tries.*) That's no good, it's far too painful. I wonder if I've broken my ankle. That will mean a visit to Casualty, x-rays and plaster casts. (*Brightening.*) I've always wondered what it would be like to have my leg in plaster. I'll make sure that everyone makes a fuss of me. James will have to carry my school bag and Helen will have to help me up and down the stairs. I really hate the way they leave me all the time – this will teach them...

She starts to cry.

.... I can hear them calling my name. (*Shouting.*) I'm over here – I'm so pleased to see you. Thank goodness you've come.

THE DEVOTED FRIEND

adapted by Jean Howell

This speech is adapted from Oscar Wilde's famous children's story.

This speech is part of a moral told by Linnet. Hard working Hans has generously supplied the covetous Miller with garden produce. But when Hans has no produce left, the Miller ceases to visit.

MILLER: There is no good in my going to see little Hans as long as the snow lasts, for when people are in trouble they should be left alone and not be bothered by visitors. That at least is my idea about friendship, and I am sure I am right. So I shall wait till the spring comes, and then I shall pay him a visit, and he will be able to give me a large basket of primroses, and that will make him so happy.

You would give him half your porridge, son, and show him my white rabbits? What a silly boy you are! I really don't know what is the use of sending you to school. You seem not to learn anything. Why, if little Hans came up here, and saw our warm fire, and our good supper, and our great cask of red wine, he might get envious, and envy is a most terrible thing, and would spoil anybody's nature. I certainly will not allow Hans' nature to be spoiled. I am his best friend and I will always watch over him, and see that he is not led into any temptations. Besides, if Hans came here, he might ask me to let him have some flour on credit, and that I could not do. Flour is one thing, and friendship is another, and they should not be confused. Why, the words are spelt differently, and mean quite different things.

Everybody can see that. Lots of people act well, but very few people talk well, which shows that talking is much the more difficult thing of the two, and much the finer thing also!

THE DEVOTED FRIEND

adapted by Jean Howell

This is another speech adapted from Oscar Wilde's famous children's story.

In this part of the moral tale, Hans is once again visited by the Miller who knows that, again, the garden has produce. But, in a very unpleasant manner, the Miller plays a trick on Hans.

MILLER: Hans, I will give you my wheelbarrow. It is not in very good repair; indeed, one side is gone, and there is something wrong with the wheel-spokes; but in spite of that I will give it to you. I know it is very generous of me, and a great many people would think me extremely foolish for parting with it, but I am not like the rest of the world. I think that generosity is the essence of friendship, and, besides, I have got a new wheelbarrow for myself. Yes, you may set your mind at ease. I will give you my wheelbarrow.

You say you can easily put it in repair as you have a plank of wood? A plank of wood! Why, that is just what I want for the roof of my barn. There is a very large hole in it, and the corn will all get damp if I don't stop it up. How lucky you mentioned it! It is quite remarkable how one good action always breeds another. I have given you my wheelbarrow, and now you are going to give me your plank. Of course, the wheelbarrow is worth far more that the plank, but true friendship never notices things like that. Pray let me see it at once, and I will set to work at my barn this very day.

Oh! It is not a very big plank, and I am afraid that after I have mended my barn-roof there won't be any left for you to mend the wheelbarrow with; but, of course, that is not my fault. And now, as I have given you my wheelbarrow, I am sure you would like to give me some flowers in return. Here is the basket, and mind you fill it quite full. Yes, quite full. Well, really, as I have given you my wheelbarrow, I don't think that it is much to ask you for a few flowers. I may be wrong, but I should have thought that friendship, true friendship, was quite free from selfishness of any kind.

THE TOOTH FAIRY

by Jeffrey du Cann Grenfell-Hill

This scene may be played equally well by a boy or girl of 8 or 9. Lou is talking to a friend in the playground.

LOU: When I lose a tooth Mum always says, "Put it in your tooth-pillow dear and the tooth fairy will come for it tonight". She made me a tooth-pillow ages ago; it's had about eight tooths in it ... I mean teeth in it ... Sometimes I let Ruth borrow it for her tooths ... I mean teeth ... It's got a little pocket and the tooth fairy comes in the middle of the night and swaps the tooth for 10p. The first thing I do when I wake up is look under my pillow for the money.

Now, that tooth-fairy has a bad memory. She doesn't always come. Sometimes I wake up and the tooth is still there. I go in to Mum's room and she says, "Don't worry, dear, she'll come tonight and leave double, just put it back." One time, I think it was the second tooth what had dropped out, it took three nights for the tooth-fairy to come... but in the end I got 30p. Mum says it's because the tooth-fairy is very, very, very old. Well, she must be if she came to Mum when *she* was 'little'. Mum lived in the Olden Days when she was a girl.

That tooth-fairy must work very hard some nights. I mean, there must be hundreds of thousands of teeth falling out of mouths all over the world. All at the same time. It must be really worrying to that fairy to have to dash from, say me in England, to maybe Japan. Mind, there might be Japanese tooth-faries. I asked Dad about this tooth-fairy, and he said she's a bit like Father Christmas, and gets around really fast, like lightning.

It's nice to have the money. But when I was rummaging in Dad's cuff-link box, I found these. (*Brings up hand, and shows something in it.*) Eight little tooths.... I mean teeth.... they don't look like his, and I haven't seen any gaps; I think I'd notice if he had eight teeth missing. Perhaps he's still waiting for the tooth fairy to come.

I'm going to lend Dad my tooth-fairy pillow, and with a bit of luck, he'll make eighty pence tonight. Won't he be pleased!

WITCHES INCORPORATED

by Nan Woodhouse

This scene takes place at the beginning of the play, Annie is an experienced White Witch, a genial lady. She lives next door to Milly, who is less pleasant.

ANNIE: (*Reading from newspaper.*) 'Magic for beginners. How to afford more capacious cauldrons, bigger and better broomsticks...' (*Continuing to read with little sounds of surprise and delight.*) OO... MM... OH! 'Enrol now for the Whatsit Academy of Witches and Wizards. Learn to make an effective spell in ten easy lessons.' Oh! Blisters, bunions, backache, boils – what a thing to matriculate in Magic!

She rises and hops around the table in delight, singing.

Oom pa pa, oom pa pa. (*Stops suddenly.*) I'll make a wall-call... Must tell Milly... silly Milly, silly Milly.

Crosses to wall and taps three times.

Oom pa pa, oom pa pa. (*Listens.*) Millicent?

Knocks again.

Where is the silly old... (*Her voice changes suddenly as Milly thumps back from her side of the wall.*) Milly! And how are you this morning, dear? (*She makes sympathetic noises.*) Oh? Mm? There, there. How often have I told you, dear – never go out on the broomstick without your hat – not in an east wind, dear, it's asking for rheumat – toothache. (*After a second.*) Tell me, dearie, have you seen the paper? Page two, 'HALLOWEEN OFFERS – MAGIC FOR BEGIN – What? (*Pause as she listens to Milly's tirade from beyond the wall.*) Not a beginner exactly... What? Yes, I do remember your enchanted elephant. No, dear... No, dear...

Thump from the other side of the wall. Annie covers her ear.

That's done it!

Annie seizes her cloak and throws it around her.

Enchanted elephants! I'll show her!

She crosses and collects newspaper. Puts fingers in her mouth and whistles loudly. A broomstick flies in, she mounts and circles the room awkwardly.

I could certainly use a new broomstick. (*She pats the broom.*) Not complaining, Bertie, but you are getting a bit long in the too... OOPS!

The broomstick shoots forward and they exit through the window.

THE OLD CURIOSITY SHOP

adapted by Jean Howell

This passage is adapted from Chapter Six of the novel by Charles Dickens. Nell has been sent to dangerous Mr Quilp asking for money for her grandfather who, unknown to Nell, has been gambling in the hope of providing for her future. His health is suffering and Nell pleads with him to take to the road.

NELL: He told me exactly what I told you, dear grandfather, indeed. Nothing more. What if we are beggars? Let us be beggars, and be happy. Dear grandfather, I am not a child in that I think, but even, even if I am, oh hear me pray that we may beg, or work in open roads or fields, to earn a scanty living, rather than live as we do now. Yes, yes, rather than live as we do now. If you are sorrowful, let me know why and be sorrowful too; if you waste away and are paler and weaker every day, let me be your nurse and try to comfort you. If you are poor let us be poor together, but let me be with you, do let me be with you, do not let me see such change and not know why, or I shall break my heart and die. Dear grandfather, let us leave this sad place to-morrow, and beg our way from door to door.

Let us be beggars. I have no fear but we shall have enough, I am sure we shall. Let us walk through country places, and sleep in fields and under trees, and never think of money again, or anything that can make you sad, but rest at nights, and have the sun and wind upon our faces in the day, and thank God together. Let us never set foot in dark rooms or melancholy houses any more, but wander up and down wherever we like to go, and when you are tired, you shall stop to rest in the pleasantest place that we can find, and I will go and beg for both.

MAKING FRIENDS

by Nan Woodhouse

The scene is a croft, the local name given to a bomb site. The time is post Second World War. Davie talks to Laurie, a nine year old neighbour.

DAVIE: My Grandad played professional football. He was an International. (*As LAURIE looks amazed.*) I'm not telling lies. Ask Mam. No, I can't play. (*He aims a competent kick at a nearby bit of stone.*) I don't want to play. I'd sooner... I'd sooner...

(*In response to suggestion from the imaginative LAURIE.*) Yeah... Yeah, I'd sooner do that. I'd sooner knock conkers off trees. And I can run. I can run fast. I can run faster than the others even without –

Mum can't get me any pumps. She can't afford boots. I could run in bare feet. I can't play Footie in bare feet. It's a barmy game, anyway. Barmy.

When I grow up I'm going to be a school teacher. I'm going to stand at the front door of my school and on the first morning I'm going to dish stuff out. I'm going to dish a pair of boots out to every kid that answers his name when I call out the register at the front door. I'm going to give out a pair of white pumps in the afternoon. Knocking off time it'll be... (*Inspired suddenly, he gazes out across the croft, smiling.*) ... tickets all round to Wembley.

MAKING FRIENDS

by Nan Woodhouse

The scene is a croft, the local name given to a bomb site. The time is post Second World War. Laurie is a small nine year old. She enters and crouches on an abandoned wooden box. She cannot sit still for long. This speech is a pretend game she more than half believes to be real.

LAURIE: The wild garden! My own wild garden! (*Suddenly, as though someone has contradicted her.*) It is, it is! You shall not take it away from me.

Silence

I can hear... I can hear a cricket. Busy little thing.

Pause.

If I sit here, on this stone, the special person may come and talk to me. (*Pause.*) Now I can hear the buzzing of a bee.

She rocks back and forth, imitating the sound of a bee. Suddenly she glances sharply to the side. Her face lights up.

There you are! (*She jumps to her feet.*) I knew you would come! You are my friend, my good, kind friend. Say that you are. Say that you are. Say it!

Oh, please don't be angry, please don't go away.

She reaches up and takes an imaginary apple from an imaginary tree.

Here! Have this apple, this lovely, golden apple – so good to eat, juicy and sweet. Now, please sit down again. I want to tell you about all the things that happen to me in that house. When it is dark they leave me alone! Alone in the dark with no candle! There are big, black crawling things with enormous faces and claws for hands and when they have been watching for a long time they creep down the walls and slide across the floor. (*Becoming very upset.*) Granny left me a light, my very own candle, but Granny has gone. Do you know where she has gone? My auntie said Granny is dead – but that is a lie. And I have not seen my Dad for such a long time! (*Suddenly she laughs.*) He sent me funny letters with animal drawings – penguins and tortoises and lions – but I haven't seen him for so long. I thought he'd come back after the war but ...

Silence.

Now I have to live with my aunt. Oh, I hate her. She is cruel. She never smiles. I hate her, I hate her!

She buries her head in her hands and sobs.

(*Suddenly peeping between her fingers.*) You are not listening to me. *Pay attention!* Oh, you are no use for a friend. Go away! Go away and leave me in my garden!

She looks around to see if the special person is still there, then runs after her to the edge of the croft calling.

But you can come again – *tomorrow!*

THE CHIMNEY SWEEP'S BOY: 1852

by Jeffrey du Cann Grenfell-Hill

The young actor should look bedraggled. He is ill-educated and we imagine him in the back-room of the chimney sweep's house. Miming a simple meal at a table might suit. The actors speaks directly to the audience.

BOY: See, I'm an orphan. 'Bandoned I was, on the Workhus steps, at Christmas time... cryin' my 'ed off I was... so they takes me in an' calls me Christmas Eaves... can't say it's a name I'd choose... But most people calls me Chris, an' that might be short for Christopher, so p'raps it ain't worth bothering on.

They works you 'ard at the Workhus; when I were just three they sends me out in the gardens stone-picking... picking up stones by the dozen... an' a right stony bit of land they built that Workhus on... Comes I'm seven an' the beagle comes an' tells the Master I got to be bound 'prentice, on the parish... an' Fred Bowles the chimney sweep wants a small un...

Now I be the smallest seven year old in that place. So the Master calls me to 'im an' 'ands me over to the beagle... an' afore I knows what's 'appening I'm taken to Fred Bowles 'ouse an' bound to 'im. You should 'ave seen 'is face... "Oh! I asks for a little un, an' I gets a midget... a veritable midget... what chimneys he shall climb... what nasty little corners he'll be able to get round..." 'E says all this 'as 'e dances 'round me, rubbin' 'is 'ands with glee.

Nasty 'e is, 'specially with a nasty little fork 'e 'as which 'e prods me with when the chimney is still 'ot, an' I don' want to go any further. "Up you goes, midget," 'e says, an' gives me a prod with 'is fork. It's cruel it is.

But I says my prayers reg'lar like, an' hopes God is with me... An' as I climbs a really 'ot un, I says "Please Lord, save me from dyin" an' when I gets to be a master chimney sweep I promises never to send little boys up red 'ot chimneys. That's what I says, an' I tells you straight, I intends to keep that promise.

THE EXAMINATION

by Penny Phillips

The stage is set with a row of chairs at a diagonal to the audience. A young person enters carrying a musical instrument, stops and calls back off stage.

ALEXANDRA: I'll be alright, Mother. Really, don't worry – it'll be easy. Mr Jones will be here very soon.

Puts music and instrument on the chairs and then looks across the room. She knocks on an invisible hatch.

Hello. Good morning I'm Alexandra Townsend. (*The ELDERLY LADY is deaf.*) Alexandra *Townsend*... yes. I'm here for my clarinet examination... No I don't want the toilet! Grade four... Clarinet... Yes.

Four. No! – not which door. But my accompanist hasn't arrived yet... My accomp... It doesn't matter... (*To herself.*) I'll be alright.

Crosses to chairs, unpacks instrument.

I'll be fine. Out you come... One – two – three – four. No! Where's my reed? (*Assembling the separate pieces of the clarinet.*) I bet I've forgotten it... Here it is. Remember to lick it, Alexandra.

Remember reeds are 50p each... Now... Where's my music?... I bet I've forgotten it. Oh. There it is... Now, Alex – you are a very good clarinettist. *You* are brilliant. You *are* brilliant. You are *brilliant!*

She blows and makes a feeble noise. She panics. She looks at her watch.

No! Where is Mr Jones? My examination is in five minutes.

She puts clarinet down – walks across to hatch – knocks on hatch – waits as an ELDERLY SECRETARY opens hatch.

Excuse me. *Alexandra Townsend.* Yes... I know my examination is in five minutes but my accompanist hasn't arrived yet. My accomp... Ohoo!

Getting very frustrated, she mimes a piano being played.

Look... the man who is playing the *peeano* for me! Yes! Piano. (*Smiles with relief, then...*) *No!* I'm not playing the piano – I'm doing a clarinet exam! I've lost my *pianist.* I'm not playing the piano, *he is!*

(*Trying to calm down.*) Look. I cannot do my examination without Mr Jones... Because he plays the *piano* for me... (*Almost in tears.*) What? He's where? He's in there waiting for me? I'm sorry.

Picks up clarinet and the music.

I'm so sorry... I am really sorry...

Picks up clarinet case and music, crossing to the door and knocking loudly.

Hello Mr. Jones

TROUBLE

by Simon Parker

Trouble is a small, bouncy, energetic dog who lives in a comfortable home and is well looked after. This speech may be performed by a girl or a boy – or, indeed, a small dog! At the start of the speech, Trouble is flopped out on the floor.

TROUBLE: (*Opening an eye.*) Oh. It's morning. It's sunny. (*With great excitement.*) Oooh! (*Jumping up.*) It's a lovely, lovely day. It's a day for... yes, it's a day for walkies. Walkies! Oooh, Mummy! Daddy! It's a day for walkies.

TROUBLE runs to the door and starts to scratch.

Come on, Mummy. Come on, Daddy. It's time for walkies! Walkies! Bother, they must still be asleep. WALKIES, MUMMY! WALKIES, DADDY!!

TROUBLE starts to bark. The door opens.

(*Jumping up.*) Hello, Mummy! Hello, Daddy! Can we go walkies? Can we? Can we? I love you, love you, love you, love you. Oh, isn't it exciting that you're awake. Play with me, Mummy. Play with me... Mummy..? Daddy...? Play with me.

TROUBLE rolls over and exposes a stomach ready to be tickled.

Look, I'm a good dog, a good dog, a very good dog, the very best dog. Tickle me, Mummy. Tickle me, Daddy.

Getting no response, TROUBLE barks again then, very disappointed, walks away.

It's not fair. They're awake, I know they're still awake. I can hear them talking. They don't want to play with me. And it's such a lovely day. Humph! Good walkies time going to waste. It's a rotten life.

TROUBLE sulks for a minute.

(*Brightening up.*) Wonder if there's any food left? Let's have a look in my bowl. (*Looking.*) Oh, yes. Yes, yes, yes. Biscuits!

TROUBLE takes a biscuit and throws it in the air.

I'm going to eat you, biscuit. Oh yes I am. (*Playing with it, batting it around the floor.*) Over there. No, over there! Got you! Ha ha, biscuit, now you're going to be eaten. You're going to be eaten good and proper.

TROUBLE eats the biscuit.

Yum. (*Suddenly hearing a noise.*) It's that man pushing paper through the door again! I'll get you! You can't push paper through my door. I'll get you!! I'll get you!!

TROUBLE runs off barking.

AT THE CIRCUS

by Mary Patrick

Marcellus, a small boy, is waiting with other Christians in a dank, dirty dungeon below the amphitheatre of the Colosseum. He knows that today, or some day soon, he and his companions will be sport for the Roman citizens who are thronging into the place – he can see the arena through a small grille in the wall. He can hear the noises of wild beasts from an adjoining dungeon.

This speech could be equally well played by a girl – in which case, she could be called Marcella

MARCELLUS: (*Looking through the grille.*) I can see the nutsellers and the flower girls getting ready. It'll be full out there, soon. You were right, Didius. It's a big day today. Do you think the Emperor will be here?

I'm not afraid, Didius. Well, that's not quite true. Are you afraid? You are? Then I suppose it's alright for me to be a little bit scared too. Do you think my mother was scared when they took her? Did you watch through the grille? I couldn't watch that day. I was younger then. It was a long time ago.

Is it really only a week? It seems like much longer. Perhaps I've grown up since then. Father always said I was growing up too quickly. Do you think it hurt Father when they crucified him on the road? He told me not to be afraid, that he was going to be with the great Spartacus, that it was an honour to be crucified with Spartacus. He said you only feel the pain for a little while and after that it's peaceful. You float away, up into the sky where it's always sunny. Not like this place. I hate it in here. Still, at least I'm not afraid of the dark any more.

Why do they hate us? What harm have I ever done the Emperor? If I was Emperor, I wouldn't want to watch us being killed by wild animals. What chance have we got against the animals? They call it sport, but I can't see the fun in it.

(*Looking out of the grille.*) The back rows are quite full now. There'll be a lot of people here today. I can see a little boy in a saffron tunic. He's about my age. He looks excited. He's excited because some of us are going to die.

Do you think it will be us today, Didius?

Will you do me a favour? Will you hold my hand?

EMMA IN 1848

by Jeffrey du Cann Grenfell-Hill

The scene is in a Victorian drawing-room. Emma, aged around 9, is sitting with her sister.

EMMA: This herring-bone stitch is so difficult, so very hard. But mama says it must be done. Look, I've embroidered Noah and his ark – that was grandmother's idea – and above it the Lord's prayer – which Papa suggested and Miss Taylor made me embroider the alphabet three times in three different sizes. This has to be the biggest sampler any girl anywhere has ever been made to do! Mama says she will have Simpkin take it into Bath to have it framed and it will hang in the schoolroom – the schoolroom! Really, Victoria, I expected her to say the morning-room at least, not the schoolroom. I shan't want to see the horrid thing *ever*, once I've done with it.

She throws it down.

It must be wonderful to be a... a... dairy-maid. A dairy-maid would be free to do as she pleased I'm sure they are never-made to sit and embroider. Think, up with the sun, ready to milk the cows and churn the milk into butter. One could gossip, one could giggle, there'd be no such thing as 'proper behaviour', I'm sure their mothers never tell them to be more lady-like. Wishful thinking.

She sighs and picks up the sampler again.

When I've finished this, mama says I must embroider my initials on two dozen handkerchiefs. *Two dozen!* Life is going to be an endless chain of embroidery. When I'm twelve, I'll have to start preparing my trousseau. Do you know what that means? Dozens and dozens of things. It can take years, a decade... *forever!*

THE COLLECTOR

by Simon Parker

Jason, a rather pompous little boy, is given a hard time by his classmates – not entirely surprisingly. He responds by being very superior and condescending.

JASON: I don't care if you don't want to talk to me. I don't want to talk to you, either. Why would I want to talk to you?

Shut up. Don't call me that.

Well, at least I've been on the *Antiques Roadshow*. I have, actually. I'm going to be on the TV in March. So there.

I thought you might want to talk to me once I told you that. I don't know if I want to tell you, actually. Oh, alright. I took my Star Wars figures. I've got all hundred and thirty of them including Dog Face who was only on the screen for two seconds and the figure was only released in Canada. My Dad made a special case for them all. And I've got Star Wars shampoo and Star Wars towels and three different Star Wars duvet covers. You know that R2D2 that I swapped for my James Bond cards? The one I got from Pete Perkins? Well, it turns out to be a Japanese version. There were only two hundred of them made with that colour casing. It's worth nearly five hundred pounds. And my whole collection, all together, is worth nearly three thousand pounds. So they're going to put me on television and I'll probably become the world's leading expert on Star Wars figures and one day I'll be an expert on the *Antiques Roadshow* myself. So if you don't talk to me nicely from now on, I won't remember you when I'm famous.

What do you mean? You can't tell Pete Perkins how much it's worth. He'll kill me. Please don't tell him. You won't, will you?

I'll deny it. I'll say you're lying. I'll say I was lying. Oh no, I can't, can I? I'm going to be on TV. Look, if you promise not to tell I'll by you a Mars bar every day next week.

Please don't tell him.

THE SCARLET LETTER

adapted by Shaun McKenna

Adapted from Nathaniel Hawthorne's famous novel, the scene is a sea-shore in New England in the late seventeenth-century. Pearl is seven, the illegitimate daughter of Hester Prynne. The child's father, unknown to anyone but Hester, is the minister, Arthur Dimmesdale. Hester has been forced by the authorities to wear a scarlet 'A' for 'adulteress' on her clothing. Pearl is described by Hawthorne as a mixture of innocence and wildness, sweetness and elf-like malice.

PEARL: Look, mother. I have collected cockleshells and mussel-shells and these funny long shells. What are they, do you think?

She kneels in the sand and starts to arrange them.

I'm going to make something out of them. A pretty pattern or... I know! There! Look!

Looking up at her mother.

Why are you looking like that, Mother? Don't you like it? You have turned quite pale! It is only the letter A, Mother, just like the letter you wear on your breast. When I grow up, I shall wear a letter on my breast, just like you. What letter shall I wear? Shall I wear 'P'? P for Pearl.

She starts to sing to herself as she plays with the shells.

'P for Pearl, Pearl beyond price. P for Pearl, Pearl beyond price. P for...' Mother, why doesn't everyone wear a scarlet letter on their breast? Or even a blue letter or a brown letter. The governor could wear a gold letter, he is so grand. He could wear a 'G' for Governor. Perhaps everyone does wear a letter. Perhaps they wear it under their clothes. Why do you wear the letter A, Mother, when your name does not begin with A?

And why does the minister always press his hands to his heart as if he is in pain? Do you think he has sewn a letter to his shirt and pricked himself? That would be funny, wouldn't it?

Oh Mother, why do we have to go home? Why are you crying? I want to stay and play. Indeed, I shan't go home! I shan't. Not unless you catch me first.

She runs off.

I'M CHEESED OFF

by Jeffrey du Cann Grenfell-Hill

This speech will work equally well for a boy or girl. The young person is complaining to a friend. It can be set in a bedroom, with mime suggesting the picking up of clothes and games. Opening drawers and filing boxes can be effective.

JO: Do this! Do that! Tidy this! Clean that! It's like living in a concentration camp. I'm cheesed off! Why can't I be naturally untidy? You want to hear old bossy big-boots talking to her friends. "Oh yes," she says, "I like my children to be individuals... Do their own thing, you know. I just can't abide children with no characters – the cowed type. You know!" Oh, she does go on. Then, when she comes home it's stright up to inspect my bedroom.

Well, I admit, it is a bit... untidy... a bit messy... Just the odd ten or twelve books scattered around. The odd three or four games all out of their boxes... then two or three puzzles not quite finished... and, well, clothes look better with wrinkles, don't they? And anyway... they're MY clothes! If I want to pile them on my desk, why can't I? If I want to look a wreck, why can't I? But am I allowed to? *No!*

It's "Tidy up that bedroom, hang those clothes up, put those games away!" Mothers! Why can't they be more like Dads?

THE SECRET GARDEN

adapted by Frances Glynne

Frances Hodgson Burnett's famous story, set in Yorkshire, has always proved a popular source of scenes. In this new adaptation, orphan Mary is talking to her cousin, the invalid, Colin, all about the boy Dickon, the birds and all the other exciting adventures outdoors. Note: Don't let the Yorkshire dialect put you off. For Festival and examination purposes you could be North Eastern, Irish, Lancashire, Welsh...Just change the line "A bit of Yorkshire" to suit.

MARY: 'T's th' wind from th' moor. It comes o' sittin' on th' grass under a tree wi' Dickon an' wi' Captain an' Soot an' Nut an' Shell. It's th' springtime an' out o' doors an' sunshine as smells so grandly. (*Pauses, smiling.*) I'm givin' thee a bit o' Yorkshire. I canna talk as graidely as Dickon an' Martha can but tha' sees I can shape a bit. Doesn't tha understand a bit o' Yorkshire when tha' hears it? And tha's a Yorkshire lad thysel' bred and born! Eh! I wonder tha'rt not ashamed o' thy face. (*She begins to laugh.*) Ben Weatherstaff says I was like him, he said he'd warrant we both got the same nasty tempers. I think you are like him, too. We are all three alike, you and I and Ben Weatherstaff. He said that neither of us were much to look at and we were both as sour as we looked. But I don't feel as sour as I used to before I knew the robin and Dickon. I'll tell you about Dickon. His nose turns up and he has a big mouth and his clothes have patches all over them... But if there were a Yorkshire angel – I believe he'd understand the green things and how to make them grow and he would know how to talk to the wild creatures as Dickon does. Can I trust you? I trusted Dickon because the birds trust him. Can I trust you for sure – for sure?

Well, Dickon will come to see you tomorrow and bring his creatures with him. But that's not all. The rest is better. There is a door into the garden. I found it. It is under the ivy on the wall. (*Snapping.*) Of course you'll see it. Of course you'll live to get into it. Don't be silly! (*Very softly.*) I have seen it and I have been in. I found the key and got in weeks ago but I daren't tell you. I daren't because I was so afraid I couldn't trust you – for sure.

TADPOLES

by Dennis Conlon

This speech, either addressed directly to the audience or to an imaginary companion, is best suited to a boy. The contents are self-explanatory.

BOY: Can you guess what I'm doing? Tadpoles. Yeah, that's it. I'm eleven years old and I'm fishing for tadpoles. 'Course, they're not for me; they're for my little eight year old brother, Liam. He was here a minute ago but he got bored and cleared off. I used to come here when I was his age. Yeah, with Eddie Spence. Eddie Spence used to bring me here. I used to look up to Eddie Spence. I always wanted to be like him. He went to Berkley Grammar. I've ended up at Linnaker St. You see, his dad's an architect. My dad's as thick as a docker's sandwich.

We used to have this clock, right? It'd been on the mantelpiece for years. I think it was a wedding present or something. Anyway, Mum loved it. One day it stopped. Mum kept nagging at me dad to get it fixed but he never got round to it. Anyway, one afternoon he comes home, drunk as usual. I says to him, 'Why don't you take that clock down to the menders and get it fixed? Surprise Mum.' 'That's a good idea,' he says. He goes off to the kitchen and he brings back this brown paper bag. He takes the clock off the mantelpiece and drops it into the bag. It goes straight through and smashes into little pieces, all over the hearth. I laughed my head off. Mum went barmy.

Mind you, she's not much cleverer. My dad bought her this radio for Christmas, right? She loved it. But then the batteries ran out. Mrs Cummins next door says to my Mum, 'If you warm them batteries up, you'll get a bit more life out of 'em.' I comes home from school and there's this horrible smell. I says, 'What are you cooking, Mum?' She says, 'Nothing.' I open the over door. She's only gone and shoved the whole radio in the oven, hasn't she? It'd melted all over the oven floor.

Is it any wonder that I've ended up at Linnaker St, with parents like that? Now look at me, fishing for tadpoles at eleven years old.

Hey, wait a minute! Eddie Spence used to do this. Do you get it? I'm like Eddie Spence. I'm fishing for tadpoles, just like him. I could be like him. I could go to Berkley Grammar. I could even be an architect, if I wanted. I can do anything.

BALLET EXAM

by Penny Philips

A small girl stands on a chair, having the hem pinned by her mother. The dress is for her Grade 1 Ballet exam next week. She grumbles.

HARRIET: Why can't I do my exam tomorrow like the others in Group A?

This is the best costume I've ever had.

Moves around to face audience and sees herself in a mirror on the wall – over the audience's heads.

You will do my hair, won't you Mummy?

Mummy, you will do it like Amanda's, won't you?

MUMMY has her mouth full of pins and nudges HARRIET to turn round to be in profile to audience.

Mummeee...Ouch! OUCH! You stuck that pin in me on purpose.

MUMMY gets up and leaves the room.

Mummy – Mum – I'm sorry – I didn't mean to be rude.

HARRIET steps carefully off the chair.

Mummy, I'm sorry... All right I won't move.

Turns back into the room and stands in front of the "mirror" – the audience. Twirls and slowly does point to the side – point to the side.

(*Loudly.*) Oh Mummy, I look just right.

Moves again.

Look Mummy. Look at my pliés. (*Does them.*) I do them better than Amanda or Alison. Alison does them like this.

HARRIET does it very clumsily.

And as for Susan. She does them like this.

Does them very badly.

Mummy LOOK! (*In a very grown up voice.*) Oh why are you never here when I want you? *Mummy come and look!*

Stamps her foot and shouts.

I'm better than all of them. I should be taking the exam tomorrow. I don't need an extra week's lesson. Miss Reed is wrong. I'm ready (*She does a jeté and then twirls.*) *I'm ready.*

Phone rings.

Mummy the phone's ringing. Shall I answer it? "Hello? Harriet Marsden speaking. May I help you? Oh hello, Miss Read. Mummy's tied up at the moment. What? Amanda's ill? But I can't. I'm not ready. Oh. Goodbye Miss Read. Mummy – I'm doing my exam at 9.00 a.m tomorrow morning!!

THE CUBS' TRIP

by Jeffrey du Cann Grenfell-Hill

The scene is set behind a mini-bus on which the Cubs have travelled.

BOY: Hello Mum. Yes, we had a super time, it was terrific... Windsor Safari Park is the best place for a Cubs' outing. We all want to go again next year. Can you carry my lunch-box? I'm worn out.

I was a bit sick on the way down. Only a bit. Akela said it was because I ate my fish-paste sandwiches as soon as I got on the bus... but I was hungry... then I had the Turkish Delight bars, then a drop of Coke. Roger didn't like me being sick all over him, but I couldn't help it. It was the second can of Coke that did it. Then I was starving when we got to Windsor, so Roger gave me his cheese sandwiches which he didn't want.

What? My shoes? What happened to my shoes? Well, I know they're a bit muddy... Yes, it is up to my ankles, but I couldn't help it... It happened when Roger got a bit scratched, only a bit... he was waving his arm about... that is, outside the mini-bus... only a little bit out, like two or three fingers... and this lion came along and grabbed it... well, it wouldn't let go, so I leaned out of my window, caught the door latch and it flew open and I fell down into the mud... it wasn't too muddy and I didn't mind.

Well, then the lion made a grab for me, and I got scratched too. Look! But at least Roger got his arm in. Then Akela tried to pull me in, but fell out... well, he fell on top of me, but I managed to climb back in, so the lion scratched Akela a bit... perhaps a bit more than me... a bit... and we all want to club together to send him a Get Well Card.

Yes. We had to leave Akela at Windsor General Hospital.

It was definitely the best Cub Trip we've ever had, better than that trip we had to Clacton-on-Sea. But, gosh, I'm really exhausted.

Also published by Oberon Books in association with LAMDA:

Solo Speeches for Men (1800-1914)
ISBN: 1 84002 046 6

Solo Speeches for Women (1800-1914)
ISBN: 1 84002 003 2

The LAMDA Anthology of Verse and Prose, Vol XV
ISBN: 1 84002 120 9

The LAMDA Guide to English Literature
ISBN: 1 84002 011 3

Classics for Teenagers
ISBN: 1 84002 023 7

Scenes for Teenagers
ISBN: 1 84002 031 8

Meaning, Form and Performance
ISBN: 1 870259 74 2

First Folio Speeches for Men
ISBN: 1 84002 015 6

First Folio Speeches for Women
ISBN: 1 84002 014 8

Contemporary Scenes for Young Women (1985-2000)
ISBN: 1 84002 130 6

Contemporary Scenes for Young Men (1985-2000)
ISBN: 1 84002 141 1

The Discussion
ISBN: 1 870259 71 8

Mime and Improvisation
ISBN: 1 84002 012 1